ii

SIT-IN
HOW FOUR FRIENDS
STOOD UP
BY SITTING
DOWN

BY
ANDREA
DAVIS PINKNEY

ILLUSTRATED BY
BRIAN PINKNEY

SCHOLASTIC INC.

"We must . . . meet hate with love."

These were Dr. Martin Luther King Jr.'s words that got them started.

Four hungry friends. Eager to eat.

Each took a seat at the Woolworth's lunch counter
in Greensboro, North Carolina.

David, Joseph, Franklin, and Ezell sat quiet and still.

With hearts full of hope.

With Dr. King's words strong and close.

They were college students with a plan.

It was February 1, 1960.

3

They didn't need menus.
Their order was simple.
A doughnut and coffee,
with cream on the side.
Woolworth's was busy,
so the friends waited.
Patiently. Silently.
Without a fuss.
They were the only
black kids at the counter.

David, Joseph, Franklin, and Ezell
sat while everyone else got served.

At first, they were treated like
the hole in a doughnut — invisible.

Others tried to ignore them.
The waitress watched and refused them.

This was a sign of the times:

WHITES ONLY.

This was the law's recipe for segregation.
Its instructions were easy to follow:
Do not combine white people with black people.
Segregation was a bitter mix.

Now it was the friends' turn to ignore and refuse.
They *ignored* the law, and *refused* to leave until they were served.
Those kids had a recipe, too.
A new brew called integration.

It was just as simple:

Combine black with white to make sweet justice.

For them, integration was better than any chef's special.
Integration was finer than homemade cake.
Integration was a recipe that would take time.

So David, Joseph, Franklin, and Ezell sat quiet and still. With hearts full of hope. With Dr. King's words strong and close:

"Be loving enough to absorb evil."

They sat straight and proud. And waited. And wanted. A doughnut and coffee, with cream on the side. After sitting and waiting and wanting, a police officer came. But the four friends wouldn't leave.

The police officer didn't know what to do.
The students were doing nothing wrong.
No crime in sitting.
No harm in being quiet.
No danger in looking hungry.
The officer left the lunch counter
without doing anything.

The Woolworth's man turned off the lights.
He announced, "Woolworth's is closed."
So the customers left,
including the four friends,
who went home to dinner,
where they were served first.

News had already spread about the sit-in.
David, Joseph, Franklin, and Ezell
got their names in the paper.
The next day, February 2, 1960,
more students showed up
at the lunch counter.

Sitting still for what was right.

No reservations needed at Woolworth's.

The students seated themselves.

They were dressed in their best clothes.

They were polite and determined.

No guesswork for the waitress.
The young people knew the menu by heart.
They ordered. No food came.
So they sat. In silence.
And waited. And wanted.
A doughnut and coffee, with cream on the side.

The waitress reminded them:

WHITES ONLY.

But those kids wouldn't budge.
They didn't move.
Until they were served, they refused.
All they wanted was some food.
A doughnut and coffee,
with cream on the side.

To pass the time, the students
read their schoolbooks.
They wrote in their journals.
They finished their homework.
They didn't need to read the menu,
so they studied for tomorrow's test.

What had started in Greensboro
spread faster than a grease fire.
There were lunch counter protests in
Hampton, Virginia; Nashville, Tennessee;
Montgomery, Alabama; Atlanta, Georgia;
and many other southern towns.
If lunch counters could go from
WHITES ONLY to ALL WELCOME,
if segregation could turn to integration,

**if black people and white people
could break bread together,
everyone would pass the test.**

Everybody would score high.
A+ with that coffee and cream on the side.

But many folks were not motivated to make that grade.
As the sit-ins grew, angry people gave the students
a big dose of hatred — served up hot and heaping.
Coffee, poured down their backs.
Milkshakes, flung in their faces.
Pepper, thrown in their eyes.
Ketchup — not on the fries, but dumped on their heads.
They yelled at the students.
"We don't serve your kind!"
"Go home!"
"Goodbye!"

The students wanted to lash out, but couldn't.
They wanted to strike back, but didn't.
Sitting still was *so hard*.

Practicing peace while others showed hatred was tougher than any school test.

Now there were news cameras filming the sit-ins.
And viewers at home watching it all on TV.
The students were more determined than ever
to show the world the true meaning of peace.
So they sat. In silence.
With hearts full of hope.
With Dr. King's dream true and close.
These were the words that kept them going:

"We must meet violence with nonviolence."

The students sat proud and still.
And waited. And wanted.
A doughnut and coffee,
with cream on the side.

Soon the sit-ins grew bigger and wider.

White students joined their black friends to protest the unfair treatment by restaurant owners who would not serve food to black patrons. They also opposed segregated libraries, buses, parks, and pools.

With so many students gathered,
people got scared there would be fighting.
They were afraid of all those youngsters
grouped together for a cause.
Even though the students were committed
to peace, the police now took action.
They accused the students of loafing.

They arrested them.

They took them to jail.

The students didn't resist.

They didn't fight.

Instead, they sang freedom songs — to keep the peace.

They held Dr. King's words steady and close:

"Demonstrate . . . calm dignity."

Soon folks were so busy arguing about who was right and who was wrong, that they stopped going to Woolworth's and other segregated places. Some shops were forced to integrate to keep their businesses alive. But the struggle was far from over.

In April, an activist named Ella Baker organized a student leadership conference at Shaw University in North Carolina to help the young demonstrators.

With Ella, the students formed the Student Nonviolent Coordinating Committee — SNCC.

Inspired by Dr. King, they came up with powerful words of their own. These are the words that became the SNCC slogan:

We are all leaders.

When President John F. Kennedy got a taste of
SNCC's integration, he didn't sit in; he stepped in!
On June 11, 1963, the president went on TV.
He urged Americans to treat each other fairly.

He then told Congress to take action against segregation.

This became the Civil Rights Act of 1964.

On July 2, 1964, President Lyndon B. Johnson made the act a law.

It banned segregation in public places.

The hard work and courage of those brave students paid off.

They had taken a bite out of segregation.

Now it was time to savor equality.

Now they were ready for a big sip of freedom.

Their order was simple:

A double dose of peace, with nonviolence on top. Hold the hate. Leave off the injustice.

Now the students had the right recipe for integration.
The steps were easy to follow:

1. Start with love.

2. Add conviction.

3. Season with hope.

4. Extra faith to flavor.

5. Mix black people with white people.

6. Let unity stand.

7. Fold in change.

8. Sprinkle with dignity.

9. Bake until golden.

10. Serve immediately.

Makes enough for all.

After weeks of sitting — when their backsides ached.
After months of being still — when their feet fell asleep.
After years of praying for laws to change.
When they were so hungry for equality.
The young people finally got what they ordered.
It was worth the wait.
It was served to them exactly how they wanted it — well done.

And oh, integration sure tasted good.

Those courageous young people enjoyed every bit.

They came back to Woolworth's for seconds and thirds, and for many helpings after that.

When the sit-ins were all done, the students left a big tip:

A doughnut and coffee, with cream on the side, is not about food — it's about pride.

These were the words that filled them up.

Civil Rights Timeline

The Greensboro sit-ins were one of many events that comprised a time in America's history known as the Civil Rights Movement, a series of happenings in which people came together to end racial discrimination.

Here is a timeline of important civil rights moments
that came before and after the Greensboro sit-ins,
and that led to equality among people.

1954   **May 17:** The Supreme Court rules segregation in public schools unconstitutional in the landmark case *Brown v. Board of Education of Topeka, Kansas*. This ruling allows black and white children to attend school together.

1955   **December 1:** Rosa Parks, an African American seamstress, refuses to give up her seat to a white passenger at the front of a segregated bus in Montgomery, Alabama. Rosa's bravery sparks the Montgomery Bus Boycotts, during which African American citizens refuse to ride city buses for more than one year. On December 21, 1956, buses become desegregated after a Supreme Court ruling.

1957   **January–February:** Dr. Martin Luther King Jr. helps establish the Southern Christian Leadership Conference (SCLC), and becomes its first president. The SCLC serves as a driving force in the Civil Rights Movement, using nonviolence as its basis.

September: Nine black students in Little Rock, Arkansas, enroll in Central High School despite being barred from entry by Arkansas Governor Orval Faubus. When President Eisenhower sends in the National Guard, the students, who come to be known as the "Little Rock Nine," are allowed to enter.

1960 **February 1:** The Greensboro sit-ins begin.

April: Ella Baker helps found the Student Nonviolent Coordinating Committee (SNCC) at Shaw University.

July 25-26: Woolworth's in Greensboro is desegregated.

1961 **May 4:** "Freedom Rides" start when more than 1,000 student volunteers, both black and white, travel on buses throughout the South to test laws that prohibit segregation. Supported by SNCC and the Congress on Racial Equality (CORE), the students are often met by violence.

1962 **October 1:** President John F. Kennedy sends thousands of federal troops to help drive back angry mobs at the University of Mississippi, where James Meredith is the first African American student to register.

1963 **April 16:** After being arrested and put in jail during a protest in Birmingham, Alabama, Dr. Martin Luther King Jr. writes his "Letter from Birmingham Jail" in which he underscores the importance of justice.

May 2–4: Thousands of schoolchildren in Birmingham, Alabama, march in the Children's Crusade, a protest of the arrest and jailing of Dr. Martin Luther King Jr.

August 28: Dr. Martin Luther King Jr. delivers his world-famous "I Have a Dream" speech while hundreds of thousands of listeners gather at the Lincoln Memorial as part of the March on Washington.

1964 **July 2:** The Civil Rights Act of 1964, which outlaws racial segregation in schools and public places, is signed into law by President Lyndon B. Johnson.

A Final Helping

Photo: © The Granger Collection.

Pictured here, left to right, Joseph McNeil, Franklin McCain, William Smith, and Clarence Henderson, who sat at the Woolworth's lunch counter on the second day of the sit-ins.

David Leinail Richmond, Joseph Alfred McNeil, Franklin Eugene McCain, and Ezell A. Blair Jr. (now known as Jibreel Khazan), were students at North Carolina Agricultural and Technical State University, a historically black college. Frustrated by segregation and eager to bring about a change, they sparked a series of sit-ins that lasted for a period of years, and spread from the South to the northern and western states throughout America. By August 1961, more than 70,000 people took part in sit-ins. They were black and white, men and women, young and old, all passionate about the cause for equal rights.

These sit-ins closely followed Dr. Martin Luther King Jr.'s strong belief in bringing about social change through nonviolence. Dr. King's conviction in the peaceful resolution of conflicts was inspired by the teachings of Indian leader Mahatma Gandhi, who believed that freedom could be won with peace.

Dr. King carried this message publicly when he outlined the nonviolent protest approach as a means to guide participants in the Montgomery Bus Boycotts of 1955 and 1956. Dr. King's words served as guides for future protests, marches, rallies, and the sit-ins that began in Greensboro, North Carolina. Some disagreed with Dr. King's philosophy, though many embraced its value in moving civil rights forward.

Ella Baker, an activist employed by the National Association for the Advancement of Colored People (NAACP), worked alongside Dr. King on several civil rights initiatives. With Dr. King and the Southern Christian Leadership Conference, she organized the Crusade for Citizenship, a voter registration campaign that took place on February 12, 1958, and encouraged black people to vote.

Two years later, Ella mentored the college students who were involved in sit-ins, and helped them organize. The three-day student leadership conference that took place at Shaw University in April 1960 hosted more than two hundred students from all over the South. During the conference the students formed the Student Nonviolent Coordinating Committee (SNCC) to keep the cause for equality pressing onward.

In June 1960, Ella wrote an article for the *Southern Patriot* newspaper, which said:

". . . sit-ins and other demonstrations are concerned with something much bigger than a hamburger or even a giant-sized Coke . . . Negro and white students, North and South, are seeking to rid America of the scourge of racial segregation and discrimination — not only at lunch counters, but in every aspect of life."

One of the most enjoyable parts of writing about real-life events is the research involved and the details this research reveals. Like life itself, history in the making is not a perfect science, and interviews and oral histories of the Greensboro sit-ins vary on the details. But thanks to these oral histories, and information gathered from the International Civil Rights Center & Museum in Greensboro, North Carolina (an institution devoted to preserving the memory of the Greensboro sit-ins), it was intriguing to learn about so many important aspects of the February 1960 protests, including that the friends actually ordered a doughnut and coffee when they sat down at the Woolworth's counter.

During the sit-ins, the student demonstrators left Woolworth's each evening and returned the following day. The first set of four friends — David, Joseph, Franklin, and Ezell, who became known as the "Greensboro Four" — sat down on February 1, 1960. On February 2, 1960, more students joined the protest, including two young men named Clarence Henderson and William Smith, pictured here with Franklin McCain and Joseph McNeil. This was the beginning of a groundswell of friends, coming together, making a difference, changing the world.

Andrea Davis Pinkney

For Further Enjoyment

Altman, Susan. *Extraordinary African-Americans.* New York: Children's Press, 2001.

Boyd, Herb. *We Shall Overcome.* Naperville, IL: Sourcebooks, 2004.

Carson, Clayborne, David J. Garrow, Gerald Gill, Vincent Harding, and Darlene Clark Hine. *The Eyes on the Prize Civil Rights Reader: Documents, Speeches, and Firsthand Accounts From the Black Freedom Struggle.* New York: Viking Penguin, 1991.

Carson, Clayborne and Kris Shepard. *A Call to Conscience: The Landmark Speeches of Dr. Martin Luther King Jr.* New York: Warner Books, 2001.

Cobb, Charles E., Jr. *On The Road to Freedom: A Guided Tour of the Civil Rights Trail.* Chapel Hill, NC: Algonquin Books, 2008.

Eyes on the Prize: America's Civil Rights Movement. Henry Hampton. Blackside, Inc. DVD. PBS Video, 2006.

Kasher, Steven. *The Civil Rights Movement: A Photographic History, 1954–1968.* New York: Abbeville Press, 1996.

Levine, Ellen. *Freedom's Children: Young Civil Rights Activists Tell Their Own Stories.* New York: G. P. Putnam's Sons, 1993.

Rochelle, Belinda. *Witnesses to Freedom: Young People Who Fought for Civil Rights.* New York: Puffin Books, 1997.

Seeger, Pete and Bob Reiser. *Everybody Says Freedom: A History of the Civil Rights Movement in Songs and Pictures.* New York: W. W. Norton & Company, 2009 reissue.

Wexler, Sanford. *An Eyewitness History of the Civil Rights Movement.* New York: Facts on File, 1993.

Williams, Juan. *Eyes on the Prize: America's Civil Rights Years, 1954–1965.* New York: Viking Penguin, 1988.

WEBSITES*

African American Odyssey: The Civil Rights Era • *http://memory.loc.gov/ammem/aaohtml/exhibit/aopart9.html*
A comprehensive look at African American history, from slavery through the Civil Rights era.

Facing History and Ourselves • *http://www.facinghistory.org/resources/facingtoday/23*
Learn how the Civil Rights Movement relates to civil rights issues today.

From Slavery to Civil Rights: A Timeline of African-American History • *http://memory.loc.gov/learn/features/civilrights/flash.html*
A timeline of African American history including letters, photographs, and descriptions.

Greensboro Sit-ins: Launch of a Civil Rights Movement • *http://www.sitins.com/index.shtml*
Rich with information about the Greensboro sit-ins, including a timeline, photographs, and videos.

The Martin Luther King, Jr. Research and Education Institute • *http://mlk-kpp01.stanford.edu* and
http://mlk-kpp01.stanford.edu/index.php/resources/article/king_online_encyclopedia1/
Highlights Dr. Martin Luther King Jr.'s life and the initiatives he inspired.

Powerful Days in Black and White • *http://www.kodak.com/US/en/corp/features/moore/mooreIndex.shtml*
Photojournalist Charles Moore offers a visual journey of the Civil Rights era through photographs from the time period.

Telling America's Story: The U.S. Civil Rights Movement • *http://photos.state.gov/galleries/usinfo-photo/39/civil_rights_07/index.html*
Photographs and descriptions of key events in civil rights.

We Shall Overcome: Historic Places of the Civil Rights Movement • *http://www.nps.gov/history/nr/travel/civilrights/*
Photos and descriptions of historic places in the Civil Rights Movement.

Voices of Civil Rights • *http://www.voicesofcivilrights.org/*
Experience personal accounts of America's struggle for equality.

*Source: Selected by the Association for Library Service to Children (ALSC) Great Websites Committee.

Acknowledgments

To Rebecca Sherman —A. D. P. & B. P.

Exceeding thanks to: Liza Baker, Liz Casal, Melanie Chang, Adrienne Davis, Pam Gruber, Patti Ann Harris, Alvina Ling, Melanie Sanders, Andrew Smith, Victoria Stapleton, and Megan Tingley.

Special thanks to the following individuals and institutions for their continued research assistance: Association for Library Service to Children (ALSC); Brooklyn Public Library, Central Branch; Steven Diamond, photo editor; Amelia Parker, director of the International Civil Rights Center & Museum, Greensboro, North Carolina; Schomburg Center for Research in Black Culture; Elizabeth Segal; National Museum of African American Heritage and Culture, Smithsonian; Syracuse University; Jennifer Vilaga.

Andrea Davis Pinkney is the author of many acclaimed picture books and young adult novels, and she received a Coretta Scott King Book Award Author Honor for *Let It Shine: Stories of Black Women Freedom Fighters*. She is a children's book editor at a major publishing company.

Brian Pinkney has illustrated numerous books for children, including two Caldecott Honor books, and he has written and illustrated several of his own books. Brian has received the Coretta Scott King Book Award for Illustration and three Coretta Scott King Book Award Honor medals.

Andrea and Brian are a husband-and-wife team who have collaborated on a number of books for children, including the Caldecott Honor and Coretta Scott King Book Award Illustrator Honor book *Duke Ellington: The Piano Prince and His Orchestra*. They live with their children in New York City.

The artwork was prepared on Arches 300lb rough paper with watercolors and India ink.
The text and display type were set in Serifa. Book design by Patti Ann Harris and Liz Casal.

Text copyright © 2010 by Andrea Davis Pinkney. Illustrations copyright © 2010 by Brian Pinkney.
Cover copyright © 2010 by Hachette Book Group, Inc. All rights reserved.
Published by Scholastic Inc., 557 Broadway, New York, NY 10012,
by arrangement with Little, Brown and Company, a division of Hachette Book Group, Inc.
Printed in the U.S.A.

ISBN-13: 978-1-338-62740-4
ISBN-10: 1-338-62740-6

1 2 3 4 5 6 7 8 9 10   40   28 27 26 25 24 23 22 21 20 19

Scholastic Inc., 557 Broadway, New York, NY 10012